Alex Star

Written by Kerrie Shanahan

Illustrated by Ian Forss

Flying Start
to Literacy®

Contents

Chapter 1:
Alex is inspired

"What's this?" said Alex, as she flicked through her grandpa's old scrapbook.

"It's a photo from my basketball days," said Grandpa.

"Wow, you were good," said Alex. "I want to play basketball for the Sharks at school, but Nina says I'm too short. She's the best player on the team."

"Don't listen to her," said Grandpa.
"Speedy Smith was the best player on my
team and he was the shortest player."

Later that week, Alex tried out for the Sharks.

Mr Hall blew his whistle. "Let's get started," he said. "Show us your stuff, Nina."

Nina took off, dribbling up the court.

"Well done, Nina," said Mr Hall. "Next!"

Alex was up next.

"What are you doing here, Shortie?"
said Nina, as she walked off the court.

"I'm playing basketball," said Alex.

"Don't worry about her," said Carla, Alex's
best friend. "It doesn't matter how tall
you are."

The girls showed Mr Hall their skills,
and then they played a game. Alex tried
her best, but she didn't get much of the ball.

After the game, Mr Hall read out the
names of the girls who made the team.
Alex wasn't one of them.

"Bad luck, Shortie," said Nina. "Maybe
you'll grow taller before next season."

"Don't listen to her," said Carla. "I thought you were great."

Alex smiled. Carla was always saying nice things.

"Hey Alex," called Mr Hall. "Can I talk to you?"

Chapter 2:
A second chance

After school, Alex went to Grandpa's house.

"Well?" said Grandpa. "Did you get in?"

"No," said Alex. "But Mr Hall said I could be a fill-in player. I can train with the team, but I won't get much game time. I don't know if I want to be a fill-in player because Nina will tease me."

"If you like basketball, do it," said Grandpa. "I can help you if you like."

So, every Monday after school, Alex trained with the Sharks. They did drills and practised games.

Then, every Wednesday after school, Alex went to Grandpa's house. Grandpa got Alex to dribble the ball around pot plants he had set up.

Around and around she went, using her left hand and then her right hand.

"This will help you to move quickly around players," said Grandpa.

One Wednesday afternoon, Alex looked upset.

"What's wrong?" asked Grandpa.

"My shooting's getting better and I'm much faster," said Alex. "But I'm still short. And there's nothing we can do to change that!"

"It's not about being tall or short," said Grandpa. "It's about being able to jump. If you run up and down the stairs five times a day, you'll get stronger and soon you will be able to jump higher."

Alex wasn't sure, but she didn't want to disappoint Grandpa.

Chapter 3:
Time to step up

The season went by quickly and Alex trained very hard. Every week, she watched her team and cheered and clapped.

The Sharks made it into the finals. They were playing the Lions.

On the morning of the game, Mr Hall
called Alex.

"Alex," he said. "Two of the girls are sick
and can't play. If we lose one more player,
we might need you as a substitute."

"Okay," said Alex.

Her heart beat with excitement.

It was a tight game. The Sharks were playing a great team game and so were the Lions. The Lions were tall, but the Sharks were fast. Both teams shot basket after basket.

With two minutes to go to the end of the game, the score was very close. Suddenly, a scream filled the air. Everyone stopped.

It was Nina. She had fallen and was on the floor holding her ankle.

"Time out," called Mr Hall.

"Alex," said Mr Hall. "We need you."

The game restarted. Alex didn't have time to be nervous!

A Lions player grabbed the ball and shot an amazing basket. The Sharks were now one point behind . . . and time was running out!

Then the Sharks took the ball up the court. Suddenly, Alex made a move. She was in the clear and the ball was passed to her.

She dribbled towards the basket, but a very tall defender stood in her way.

Bounce, bounce, left hand, right hand.
Alex went around the defender.
Then she jumped and threw the
ball high into the air . . .
Swish!
It went through the basket.

The buzzer went off.
The Sharks had won!

The crowd cheered and clapped. Alex and the other Sharks jumped around and hugged each other.

Then Alex saw Grandpa.

"Not bad for the shortest player on the court!" he said, with a very big smile.

A note from the author

From the age of eight, I have played a team game similar to basketball called netball.

I remember as a young player trying out for various netball teams – sometimes I made the team and sometimes I didn't. Whenever I missed out, I was very disappointed. At the time, I could have either given up and stopped playing or kept on trying my best. Luckily I kept trying because I still play netball today and really love it!

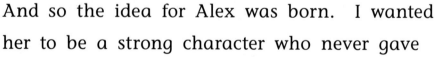

And so the idea for Alex was born. I wanted her to be a strong character who never gave

up, even when an obstacle such as her height, got in the way! I hope you can relate to some of the things that Alex goes through.